MW01205000

Dreaming in Grief

poems by

Mary Strong Jackson

Finishing Line Press
Georgetown, Kentucky

Dreaming in Grief

ACKNOWLEDGMENTS

"The Poet of Worms," Foothills Publishing, Kanona NY
"Wrens Breath" published as "Komorebi," Finishing Line Press, Georgetown,
KY
"Iksaurpok," Finishing Line Press, Georgetown, KY
"The Quiver of Cobras, The Murder of Men" published as "45," Beatlick
Press/Jules Poetry Playhouse, Albuquerque, NM
"Symbiotic Mutualism to Symbiotic Parasitism;" "Dreaming in Grief;"
"Driving Through NW Texas on Death Highway 285" Foothills Publishing,
Kanona, NY
"Witnesses" accompanied with art sculpture by R. Edward Lowe, Republic
Plaza, 11th Annual Corporate Art Show, Denver, CO 2007
"Pause" published as "Coronvirus 2020," UK Arts & Humanities Research
Council, University of Plymouth and Nottingham Trent University

Publisher: Leah Huete de Maines
Editor: Christen Kincaid
Cover Art: Mary Strong Jackson
Author Photo: Steve Smith
Cover Design: Elizabeth Maines McCleavy

Order online: www.finishinglinepress.com
also available on amazon.com

Author inquiries and mail orders:
Finishing Line Press
PO Box 1626
Georgetown, Kentucky 40324
USA

Table of Contents

For Steve

Foreword

When I read Mary Strong Jackson's *Never-ending Poems by the Poets of Everything*, I was moved by her insight about everyday things. This makes both the reading and writing of poetry accessible to everyone. In this new collection of poems about climate change, she brings this same accessibility to a dire existential threat. Every year that passes, climate change becomes more and more "an everyday thing" and more obviously a climate *crisis*.

I have been Mary's first reader for the past 4 years, and most of the poems in this collection formed in my presence. "Death Highway 285" for example, taps into an experience we had driving to Austin. It was just a month before I traveled to Stockholm to participate in a workshop on the topic of applying Complex Systems science to the Climate Crisis. We were talking about the challenges and paradoxes of global existential threats when we realized that we were dodging trucks and the potholes created by them as they beat away at this strip of highway amidst a focused fracking boom. Stopping to fuel our own tank so we could continue pushing a 3000lb, air conditioned, hunk of glass and steel across Texas was bittersweet.

I hand-carried a small number of draft copies of this collection to the Stockholm workshop. It added a much needed humanist and personal perspective to our group of scientists from around the world. It was not lost on me that I burned my entire year's carbon budget on a few weeks in Europe. We were there to discuss "what can we do?" about just such questionable choices.

The title, "Dreaming in Grief" directly references what makes this collection unique and special in this moment. When I met a friend of Mary's who was doing "grief work" around climate change, I didn't even know what that meant. That ignorance was a reflection of my own grief process. Kubler-Ross's model of the stages of grief reminds us that we will start with denial and iterate through phases of anger, bargaining, and depression before we reach acceptance. Many of us are caught in bargaining, whether through small changes like recycling or buying an electric car, or planning massive geoengineering projects. Others fall into the helplessness of depression, unable to find the energy and focus to do the things we already know to do. And of course acceptance, as we let it seep in, merely wakes us to the momentous task in front of us if we are to avoid a self-inflicted extinction level event. Being caught in this cycle is the biggest risk to not acting in time.

This is where dreaming comes in. In trying to determine when the Anthropocene began, many look at neolithic toolmaking, cave art, agriculture, city states, the harnessing of fire through steam or internal combustion, ubiquitous global transportation, nuclear energy, or our global digital communications. What these all have in common is that these are examples of collective dreaming. The evolution of ideas, society, culture and technology are collective dreams. Today a single tweet or tik-tok video may reach a significant fraction of the entire planet within a day if not seconds.

We have dreamed our way into this predicament, leveraging our knowledge, our ability to propagate it widely, and our ability to create and wield tools effectively into the kind of collective fever dream many call progress and development. This is ultimately an act of smothering ourselves in our own broken toys and their wastes.

It makes sense then that the only way out of this predicament is to dream our way out. What that means in detail is a task left to the reader, to all the readers, to all of us in this world who make choices large and small every day about who we think we are and how we will live in this world. We must do this so the world can live to support us as it has for all of history.

In this important collection of poems, Mary touches deeply on the grief now barreling down on us. This is what prevents us from beginning to dream our way out of the dreamworld of grief created by our clever minds, language and opposable thumbs. A reverse jackpot we seem dead set on winning.

Steve Smith
Otowi, New Mexico

Dreaming in Grief

What I thought was a coyote poised in mid-air
turned out to be me, limbs askew dreaming
the shape of grief.

What I thought was a rectangle of light
turned out to be the entryway to a reading
by dead women poets.

What I thought was a coat hung over a chair
turned out to be a bear offering the kind
of death I most fear.

What I thought to be the nape of a man's neck
ripe for kissing turned out to be the glistening
scar of a dolphin still caught in an acre of plastic.

What I thought was an orange dragonfly
on my car's antenna turned out to be licks
of fire from burning forests.

What I thought was my shield
and sword turned out to be a broken
yield sign.

What I thought would happen at her death
turned out to be love filling the room
making the air palpable.

Her embrace on my deep inhales—
still generous, still mothering
into death.

Wren's Breath

There is a wren's breath of silence
when a herd's last hoof comes to rest
and dust drifts back to the ground.

This same kind of quiet beckons a body
to become a bit of flotsam
filtering through trees in a sunbeam.

To nearly escape in silence
and light is enough,
to succeed, sublime.

Symbiotic Parasitism

We are tribal ticks fighting for a piece of the dog.
Reckless and abundant—too many pests
on one host. We ponder sunlight filtering
through branches, and lean over our cooking
pots deciding more pepper, a bit more thyme, yet,
we hang too long at our mother's breast, abuse

our ride on her generous hips. She tips us
sideways to see splendors—armies of saguaro,
and basins of land where red-winged blackbirds
sit atop marshy cattails. She spins us around
until we are dizzy from her gifts. Howls,
growls, skitters, and song surround us.

She attempts to warn us with flooded fields
and burnt bodies in forests, yet we respond
with a gaze at the sky as we pump gas
and shed plastic. We pave, raze, excavate,
and clear. Her distress grows. At the foot of her sick

bed, we offer toxic tinctures and foot rubs
while her lungs collapse. She speaks
of oxpecker birds riding free in exchange
for eating parasites harmful to the rhino.
She teaches even as she lies dying.

Healing

If we pressed our ears
to the ground, outer rims against
earth, inner curves a funnel
we might hear the first bellow
of a mammoth resound through time
awakening a grasshopper.
Her subtle stretch drawing
steam for the jump,
the landing.

We might hear the reverb of ancient
drum. Do you feel the beat
that taps into your feet?
The finger-snaps around the ears,
music that weaves through hair,
slides across body scars,
creates tiny shivers up a baby bird's back,
shakes snakes from winter skins,
while water whispers
over pebbles.

Together we cup the ground
press ears to earth,
gather what we already know.

A Quiver of Cobras, A Murder of Men

along a chain of bobolinks
in the wake of buzzards
amidst a bouquet of pheasants
under a gaze of raccoons

is an idle of politicians
in a climate of change
a murmuration of poor
in a shiver of homeless

flies a storytelling of ravens
a pity of doves
a glint of goldfish
with a parliament of owls

comes an army of wealth
masks of riot gear
a plutocracy of states
malignant growths of war

while a charm of finches
a dazzle of zebras
a tribe of goats
sleep with a bed of eels

under a storm of abusers
a terror of bigots
a school of shooters
and stories of enemies

a wisdom of wombats
a gulp of cormorants
an army of caterpillars
a memory of elephants

5 People at a Dinner Party

Two of us tried to remember the correct turn
off a dirt road where loose dogs of mixed heritage
questioned our presence.
Did we smell the noodle and curry soup before the door opened?
A tiny spirit in short green corduroy pants,
gray strands of hair escaping to frame her face,
stood near steaming pots stirring her magic,
warming us before we tasted.
Three of us ducked below the low viga
separating kitchen from dining room.
Stories of beginnings as far away as China
and Amsterdam, near as New Mexico,
Nebraska, and California.
All broke crusty bread, shared garden tomato
slices on thick circles of mozzarella, drizzled
with chili oil and balsamic vinegar, topped with basil.
One asked, *How does the landscape of home*
settle into one's being making a river,
ocean, mountain, prairie, or pavement
form the internal you?
Tornadoes, bridged rivers, icicled eaves,
or Santa Ana hot winds on a Saturday night
while another felt the stillness of heat.
Tea was poured and presented with a glass
jar filled with honey made from bees living
on this property. *Smell* it we are told.
Do you smell the flowers?
Imagine each flower calling a bee to land
on its bulls-eye center, live there for seconds, and return again for
more.
How does *place* make us who we are, have become?
On the prairie, one learns to see with coyote
eyes into tight expanses of space—
the speck of rabbit on a red horizon,
ghosts kneeling in snow, buffalo wallows,

hides like scalps shaping the mind
stretched on shed walls.
Will we die here? Or return from whence
we came to rest our ashes in the same
soil our pregnant mothers walked barefoot?

Driving Through NW Texas on Death Highway 285
(4.1 million barrels fracked per day)

On flatland road, heavy trucks push asphalt into welts. Cars dodge
holes the size of ottomans. White one ton dually work trucks and
semis surround my red dot of a car. Flares expel gases in red-orange
flames. Yoked to desert ground, rows and rows of workers' brown box
houses make city blocks sans city. Fresh water and brine advertised
here and there. My fingers squeeze the pump trigger. Gas fills my
tank. Trucks wall in my car whispering in gravely voices,

> "we're doing this for you"
> "we're doing this for you"
> it's what you need, it's what you want".

Grease pops from skillets as chickens fry in temporary homes.
Children make motor noises and push white toy trucks on bumpy
roads. Rabbits and coyotes pack their rabbits' feet and practiced
howls and move away from oil pumps and hydraulic frackers.

Past the pumps, past trucks pulling 40-foot trailers loaded with
60,000 pounds of pipe or drilling tools, beyond the shredded
highway, and the boxed settlements, past the fracking boom,

the land lightens its load.

Cacti with plastic bags stuck on spines become fewer. Small hills
show their rounded tops. Wide brushes of transparent clouds soothe
senses. Clumps of bushes become trees. The highway's cut exposes
million year-old rock layers of the Permian Basin. Permian, the last
period of that era.

Rain clears the palate. Greens of tall oaks unglue lids from dry eyes.
Without regrets, the car runs easy through the rain.

Difference between Gargoyles and Grotesques

From Sunday morning TV I learn,
Gargoyles come from the French "to gargle"
so have the ability to spout.
Grotesques do not gargle but hang
from their perches smiling twisted
dry grins and ghoulish grimaces.

Death comes nearer with age. It sneaks
into one's changing face. Two choices
obvious at Trader Joe's—get the odd
surgeried-face tending to look
the same on everyone or embrace
the face staring back at you in the mirror.
It's your mother's and you loved her face
at every age. Both choices hurt some.

John Steinbeck's friend, Ed Ricketts, died at 51
with so many tide pools yet to wade into and notes
on "participation", the title he thought all of his
philosophical essays could be placed under.
Make Tacos Not War said the bumper sticker,
on Highway 502. The next one—Simplify or Die.
Shall I tattoo this one on my forearm to keep me
straight as I carry plastic to recycle not knowing where
it goes and if it becomes or lays in a landfill—
what used to be called "The Dump".
My dad's sisters said they loved to shop at the dump.
We've always been throwers. Throw this, toss that,
build bigger, and bigger, until trees are gone
or dead from lack of long cold winters
making bugs multiply and chew trees to death—I don't
know if that's true. I feel it and say it
but not like His Orangeness spouting lies.
No, not like him.

He'll die one day. And so will I. Perhaps hair
dye has seeped into his brain along with other
factors, a cold mom, a crooked dad,
too much money, and Mr. Cohn's evil
persuasions.

Should we open our homes for co-op living?
With applications and trial periods like fostering
a puppy from the shelter before you adopt.
Applicants could decline your craziness
inherent in all of us, and tell you to find
another sucker to ease guilt. But
might we be enlightened by sharing
all we've got. How many loaves
and fishes does one basket feed?
A two-for-one deal—save the earth to save our souls.

This is not a song flowing from the ruby mouth
of a singer wearing used clothing moving
her hips to match the music. Long tresses
maybe black, blond, or gray. Let's give her a deep
husky voice—that's what I'd want. This is
a woman wanting to do the right
thing, or one right thing this day, and the next,
until more right things makes a difference
even a small one. Today I am a spouting
gargoyle. My friend's father used to tell him,
"Get up. Do something even if it's wrong."

Two Oars, One Direction

The woman drifts on an innocent lake
in her red rowboat with a question mark
settling down the length of her spine

asking for the routes, tips, modus
of letting go. She wants to use grace—
that vague reward given

no matter one's merit or worth.
She questions free gifts knowing
from the moment of birth

and into the bounty of being,
comes the loss of cushioned womb.
Makes being alive and losing—

all part of the un-agreed upon deal.
She looks at her oars. Calling
one love and the other loss.

The sun rises higher over the lake.
A trout ascends from water
showing black spots on pink scales

at the same time her swollen
knuckles grip the oars with less
strength.

The Poet of Worms

The poet of worms sucks dirt from his fist
thinks of the worm
its tender moist skin
much like his own tongue
he put his tongue on the worm once
just to feel   compare
to taste with no harm
the dear wiggly thing
that undulates across his palm
he exhales loud dry sighs
when he pulls them from the earth
to re-plant where they work the soil
for his vegetables that set his table
that fill his belly
seasoned by the work of the worm
soft as a tongue

The Power of Toad

A woman looks down at the stepping
stone where she is about to step
and sees a baby toad—one inch long
vulnerable as a Moses in the bulrushes—

what if she hadn't seen him?
This baby the color of sand.
Its leap too tiny to register. A heart
smaller than one gold sequin

on a flashy dress.
She squats to be near, feels
herself lifted by the power
of a tiny toad whose job is not

to distract from despair. Not to fix
this hot and burning world. Not toad's
job to unravel the meanings of home
and harbor.

It is toad's job to grow up and one day
when his body temperature is just right,
he and his fellow toads will open their
throats in song making music

on beaches, in gardens, and deserts.
Day and night the toads sing
until female toads with their own
warty desires listen and arrive.

From song comes baby toads, tiny
exporters of charm. Baby toad
disappears into tall grasses
leaving the woman

to decipher the meaning
of home and harbor.

When the Torch Won't Light

Senescence sounds
like floating face down   hair fanning from your head
wandering but attached   you come up for air   hair clings to your
face

Senescence seems
like wafting lilacs with silken
strings pulling you   the pace so dense it feels ambiguous

Senescence—slow, wooly, vague—
belongs to clockmakers who care no more for gears, pendulums,
springs, or escapement wheels

Senescence means the howling
and chugging is done   no growing   dividing
no seeking survival

Senescence, the essence
of absence

Iktsuarpok

Inuit: to go outside and check to see if anyone is coming

She goes outside to see if anyone is coming
and every time she goes, the dog rises with her.
Weather is let in time and again.
She goes out into the light.
She goes out in darkness

To see if anyone is coming.

She knows two things for sure—different animals hunt at night,
hearts loosen in the chest when the sun drops.

She hears scratching at her door
and opens it to see who's come.
It's the dog or sometimes the calico cat,
but she knows it might be miners clawing their
way to breath or that father of three   delivering pizza.
She hears his children singing for their supper
he hears them too.
She sees it in his eyes.

She goes out to see how faraway tomorrow is
to wonder what dreams will come.
Howls of coyotes crawl her spine.

She waits till shivers make her cross
back inside across the threshold
worn shiny by worry
looking first to see

if anyone is coming.

Each morning she looks for someone
then at the hill across the way
to see if its top is boiling,
to see if lava runs down the hillside

though it never has, but she checks
because she feels heat rising up her legs.

Dying In Time?

Dozens of pelicans ride rushing water.
They dash and roll near river locks,
bounce along waves then open black-tipped
wings to sail in grace across skies blue
enough to believe in forevers.

On closer viewing five pelicans crowd
on a river rock. Odd skinny-necked professors
wearing orange galoshes all with misplaced
eyeglasses. Beautiful nerds talking
physics and formulas.

The woman watches the water
from an abandoned mill turned restaurant.
Same river where logs once passed
after Frenchmen came with canoes.
After First Nation people fished without strangers.

She eats a strawberry and spinach salad
wondering how many women sat
in this spot watching birds dive for fish
thinking how lucky to be this old and die
before the earth swallows people for its own blessed rest.

Once a woman sat in this spot
wondering why men speaking French
arrived and changed her life.
Others questioned why the paper mill
closed giving them out-of-work husbands.

Another asked when fish might flourish
to feed her family again.
The woman this day sipping wine
considers if she will live to see animals
disappear one hoofed species,

one finned flipper, one howled cry,
one business suit at a time. As oceans rise,
she'll seek out a rock spire
to sit upon like a wing-less pelican
forgetting desires of increasing

her vocabulary. Thinking only of her children.

Witnesses
For Charlie and Ed

Cave echoes still resound in our ears
the stone-knapping toolmaker's rhythm
still paces our step
each of us a carrier of rememberings
a curving stroke on cave spirals
ochered handprint fitting
our fingers like a lost glove found

Past and present eyes look skyward
greet the Belt of continuity
and imagine Orion like us—hungry hunters
of infinite musings and mysteries
we unearth the bones of ancients
touch the walls they paint
to unravel our own rhythms

The wise seek answers from Bristlecone Pines
five thousand years silent
trunks twisting from hardscrabble granite
hot breathed saber-toothed tigers scratched
their bodies on scored bark

Dearest Bristlecones

Did the sky birth you like so many stars
dropping hot bits melding you to stone shards
thirsting for decades near death
drinking fire to spawn
hands fit through the wounds of your centers
are you gods of these billions of galaxies
did you raise your branches to the light in 1054

while watching in the mirrored stars
a cliff-dwelling man craft a star and crescent moon
then sign his message with painted palm and fingers
while at the same time a Chinese astrologer
halfway around the world wrote by the light
of the same luminance
What have you heard across the endless miles?
The songs of whales?   The snarling gnashing minds of war?

Bristlecone Pines

Wrap us in your wrinkled limbs
sing to us your buffalo dreams
music of a million hooves across prairies
sounding your core

we follow you ancient pines like buffalo moving in the shadows of
clouds

Coronovirus 2020

Gaia gave us canyons in reds, yellows, and pinks,
and redwoods to live among giants
so we would know *small*

know where we fit,
but we made mountains of buffalo skulls,
harpooned whale after whale for lamp oil.

If Gaia was the mother who lived in a shoe
she'd whip us all soundly and send us to bed,
but that is not her way.

She doesn't control floods filling the plains,
doesn't halt fires lapping up a koala's fur,
doesn't stop viruses from taking old men chatting on park
benches

She knows this time offers   *a pause*
to check our frantic ways
time to clear her dark-skied lungs

time to whisper to our children,
see the deer in the meadow
see how they lift their eyes
to our quiet voices and listen

Before the Pandemic 2020

My head felt like sun-hot metal on a hood of heat
when the checks and balances tipped sideways
and slipped into alien systems where there was no glossary.
Did you feel it along your storied spine when wrongs
rose up your back? Or in your gut when you heard
of the small mouse-like Bramble Cay Melomys
dying from ocean water seeping through his door,
or the last Hawaiian tree snail known as, "Lonesome George,"
dying in captivity on New Year's Day.

Then the Pandemic

God is manipulator who picks how and when you will die?
This 100 on the plane, this one tanning on the beach?
The raccoon and the fox face off about the wearing of masks.
The fox's anger sends the smell of red into the atmosphere.
If you open your ears to death rates,   numbers become
palpable and you count everything—the stairs you climb, the streets
you cross, the days you've been home, the letters in Happy Birthday.
God is not a manipulator, she lets you die when you do.
The virus is a devil of a problem.
A boogeyman dropped in to see what shape our shape is taking.
Maybe the boogeyman brought the virus, because we've been too
dumb to scare—WARMING WARNING WARMING WARNING.
We fight for points not for understanding.
The disheartened soul of the earth shutters.
God or boogeyman needs to shake the rug of us clean.
Meerkat continues to guard the little ones. She could be our example,
but again the dumb thing.
Two ways to go with this virus—rack up points for idiocy or love your
brother and sister as you love yourself, and love yourself better than
ever.
America trips, stumbles, rolls on for now.

Another Black Man Dies from Police Brutality

Some of the country takes a knee.
Deniers will say the world is not pear-shaped.
Catch your breath, you always catch your breath until that one time.
If dying could be like going to bed after a hard life's work,
grateful for your pillow and the feel of sheets.
George Floyd, Minneapolis, Minnesota. Died, face pressed on cement.
The world is not pear-shaped. It is the shape of sorrow.
A knee on your neck, a rope in a tree, history does rhyme.
Sorrow is colored white.
I can't scrape my sorry color off, like shame it lives deeper.
My white teenagers went to parks, walked to stores, drove a car,
I never dropped to my knees each night they left the house,
never prayed a cop would not stop them, threaten, beat, or kill them.

Last words, "I can't breathe" and still the knee pushed down,
while 3 more straightened the badges on their chests

Reverse Jackpot

The yoga man on my screen says,
"Bone Breath. Breathe into your bones."
Ninth rib, thigh, and spine. Biopsy done.
Her doctor says, "Be prepared."

Yoga man says, "Crouch like a cougar. We
are all animals."
No animal waits to hear what kind of cells
divide before she growls, pounces, bites.

Yoga man," Lie on your side,
make a pillow with your curled arm,
relax the jaw" *as if this is possible.*
"Reach your arm up, press
an imaginary wall like a mime,

look past your raised hand."
Past my raised hand is a prize
pandemic to the world's gut. And
a personal punch added for the jackpot.

TV woman says, "Quarantiners sing from windows.
Elk eat landscaped leaves on city
trees, and recline in grassy medians,
mountain goats gaze in store windows.

Whales' cortisol levels drop
as fewer ships vibrate ocean waters."
Still we wait with stomachs holding
the blow from the double punch.

Doctor says, "If, then, several
favorable factors for long-term survival."
Covid 19 hangs low overhead,
a generous lottery sharing droplets

by chance like cancer.
TV Doctors say, "Wear masks if you leave the house."
The president says, "Not for me."
Emily Dickinson says,

"Hope is the thing with feathers—
that perches in the soul—..."

For Wee Children Generations Beyond
For Mya and Alex

She listened for glaciers rolling over
asked who will be forgotten?

Who will say your name when you are gone?
Can you love someone three generations beyond?

If this night friends could sit on her bed
for a bit they might pray to the sky

asking that it stay blue until fireflies
light summers forever and rains

make melodies outside windows
for all wee children generations beyond.

Slow Emergency

There is kind of slow with pandemics and climate crises

I've risen on many mornings in so many seasons
my long ago long marriage seems short-lived

There is time if one lives past 50—
no excuse for incompletions
I find something supernatural about getting
what one wants even as we learn
it wasn't   or is for the time
things unfold as they must   how could they not

if each breath comes on cue

When CoVid becomes forgotten like a pox
to inoculate
                    or the storm blows down the fence but not the
house

will I kiss with more meaning
look back
at this time with gratitude
for rattles and hisses,
                    leave threats of death under a rock
                    like the extra key for seeming

emergencies

dangerous colors of ambition
the seriousness of fast and slow

timekeepers keep their charms
in one drawer and their winding
tools in another, when they slip
and the clock spins it may land on your half-hour

to experience what you never expected
of course you didn't because you   are who you are

and some things are not meant for you

the key has gone missing   so has the rock

then you see they are and always were
you think more about the "luck of the draw"
or "making your own destiny" and know
they are ideas built of smoke
and genetics   hard to grasp what   drifts
or is unseen

Mary Strong Jackson's beginnings were formed between wooden church kneelers and bar stools. Born to an Irish mother who read from a steady stack of library books, and a truck driver father who cared little for the written word. She comes from tornadoes, buffalo wallows, ruby and topaz sunsets of Western Nebraska. Raised in Nebraska, Mary also spent short but important periods in Washington and Oregon. As a social worker, she was employed in Nebraska, New Mexico, and England. Before getting her bachelor's degree in social work and an M.ED, she began writing poetry at her kitchen table as a stay-at-home mother of three. Poetry transformed mundane daily chores into validations of her life. As a social worker her career focused on adults, foster children, and their parents with diagnoses of mental illness. She facilitated a poetry and writing group for 5 years at The Life Link Santa Fe Clubhouse and Wellness Center, a psycho-social rehabilitation facility for adults with mental illness and/or substance abuse. Mary supervised staff and all other programs at this facility. As a poet and a social worker, her desire to give voice to those with mental illness resulted in a collaboration with clients in the creation of *Singing Under Water*, a book of poetry and prose. Mary's chapbook titles are *From Other Tongues, The Never-Ending Poem by the Poets of Everything, Witnesses, No Buried Dogs, Between Door and Frame,* and *Clippings*. In 2005, Mary was chosen to participate in a Nebraska Educational Television program featuring United States Poet Laureate, Ted Kooser. Mary resides in New Mexico near Otowi Bridge on the Rio Grande.